FROM FEW TO
Many

From Few to To *Many*

HOW TO GET MORE OF WHAT YOU HAVE

BRIGHT ADDAI

Many people desire to handle big things in life but they take their minds off effectively managing the few resources that are available to them. From Few to Many seeks to enlighten you on how to become profitable and command more resources.

To …
The great men and women whose lives, messages
and books have caused a paradigm shift in the way I
manage the blessings of God on my life. I salute you all
for your input in my life and ministry.

My friends and colleagues in ministry and eslewhere who
challenged me to not despise the days of little beginnings

ACKNOWLEDGEMENT

I extend my utmost thanks to my Maker, God Almighty, for His munificent mercies and grace. He has blessed me with the ability to express my thoughts for others to learn from and I do not take this privilege lightly.

I would also like to express sincere gratitude to Rev. and Mrs. Frank Ababio and the entire leadership of Believers Baptist Church International - Atlanta, Georgia for their moral and spiritual support. May the Lord reward your labour and grant your heart desires.

Special thanks to Ps.Dr Jacob Ofori-Kuragu(Late),Rev. and Mrs. Albert Addai, Rev. and Mrs. Simon Ampofo, Mr. Earl Ofori-Atta, Rev.Jerry Owusu Adjinah, Rev. Raymond Nkrumah, Rev.Joseph Akorful, Rev.Michael Andrews, Rev.Andy Mensah, Rev.Mrs Vida Asare,

Elder Nana Kusi Appiah, Mr. and Mrs. Seidu, Pastor Emmanuel Osei Asibey, Pastor K.B.Tenkorang,Pastor Edwin Dzor, Pastor Maxwell Oppong Adjei, Ransford Eddy-Mensah, Isaac Clad and his editing team for their mentorship, counselling, spiritual and moral support as I grew up to realize and maximize my potential.Thank you all.

CONTENTS

INTRODUCTION

The thesis of this book is based on the principles gleaned from the Biblical Parable of talents.

"For the kingdom of heaven is like a man travelling to a far country, who called his own servants and delivered his goods to them. And to one he gave five talents, to another two, and to another one, to each according to his own ability; and immediately he went on a journey. 'Then he who had received the five talents went and traded with them, and made another five talents.' And likewise, he who had received two gained two more also. But he who had received one went and dug in the ground, and hid his lord's money.

"After a long time the lord of those servants came and settled accounts with them." So he who had received five talents came and brought five other talents, saying, 'Lord, you delivered to me five talents; look, I have gained five more talents besides them. "His lord said to him, 'Well done, good and faithful servant; you were faithful over a few things, I will make you ruler over many things. Enter into the joy of your lord. 'He also who had received two talents came and said, 'Lord, you delivered to me two talents; look, I have gained two more talents besides them.'"His lord said to him, 'Well done, good and faithful servant; you have been faithful over a few things, I will make you ruler over many things. Enter into the joy of your lord.

"Then he who had received the one talent came and said, 'Lord, I knew you to be a hard man, reaping where you have not sown, and gathering where you have not scattered seed. And I was afraid, and went and hid your talent in the ground. Look, there you have what is yours.'"But his lord answered and said to him, 'You wicked and lazy servant, you knew that I reap where I have not sown, and gather where I have not scattered seed. So you ought to have deposited my money with the bankers, and at my coming I would have received back my own with interest. Therefore, take the talent from him, and give it to him who has ten talents.

'For to everyone who has, more will be given, and he will have abundance; but from him who does not have, even what he has will be taken away. And cast the unprofitable servant into the outer darkness. There will be weeping and gnashing of teeth. 'When the Son of Man comes in His glory, and all the holy angels with Him, then He will sit on the throne of His glory. All the nations will be gathered before Him, and He will separate them one from another, as a shepherd divides his sheep from the goats. "And He will set the sheep on His right hand, but the goats on the left. Then the King will say to those on His right hand, 'Come, you blessed of My Father, inherit the kingdom prepared for you from the foundation of the world. (Matthew 25:14-34 NKJV)

CHAPTER ONE

According to Your Ability

*But to each one of us grace was given according
to the measure of Christ's gift.*
—Ephesians 4:7

Everyone on earth has the ability to do something. Whether it's in leadership, management, science, business, law, teaching, and/or pastoring, you have a unique ability but the danger that often confronts us is the temptation to compare our abilities with those of others, counting what we have as inferior. One of the chief aims of the enemy is to let you undervalue yourself and rob you of the gifts and talents that God has given to you. The onus is on you to respect and work with whatever ability you have and to this the Apostle Paul reminds us that each of us has been given grace (God's enabling power) according to His measure.

In the parable of the talents, the master gave out talents to each of his servants according to their ability meaning he knew what they were capable of doing with those talents. In the same way God knows what we can do and cannot do thus He grants to each of us gifts, talents and resources according to the measure of His grace upon us.

Manufacturers of products know what their products can do because they brought it into existence and this is the same with our Creator who wired us with exceptional abilities to help us fulfil our purposes in life.

When we were in primary school, our teachers gave us assignments and examined us according to our level or grade. We only got promoted or qualified to the next grade when we passed these assignments and exams. God applies the same principle to us when it comes to our abilities; we get promoted when we pass the test of engaging our abilities in the art of trading.

What abilities or talents have you been entrusted with? Are you using them or are you trying to find out how better your abilities are as compared to others. Be mindful of this fact, that, everything you will ever do and become is dependent on how well you use your God given abilities.

Three basic skills you need

The word ability also connotes skill, which is the learned capacity to carry out pre-determined results often with the minimum outlay of time, energy, or both. That is something that requires training to do. People need a broad range of skills in order to contribute to a modern economy and take their place in the technological society of the twenty-first century. I believe the skill of learning to learn, reading and problem solving are very crucial for our time if we are to make any meaningful impact tomorrow.

Learning to learn

Learning is an integral part of everyday life. The skill of knowing how to learn is a must for everybody and is the key to acquiring new skills and sharpening the ability to think through problems. It opens the door to other learning. Study smarter not harder. A secondary benefit of learning how to learn is that it empowers the learner's ability to develop a measurable task repeatedly. In the parable, one of the key skills that the servant who was given one talent probably lacked and could not use was the skill of learning to learn. Because it is probable he never made learning either from his own experiences or from those of others a part of his life thus he was afraid to trade with the talent. However, the others I believe were individuals who knew how to learn or follow the experiences of others and this made them succeed in their trade. If we are going to succeed tomorrow we must be learners either from our daily experiences or from the experiences of others. One great man puts it this way, Education, in the deepest sense is continuous and lifelong and in essence unfinishable. What we think we already know is often less helpful than the desire to learn. Finally the Apostle Paul emphatically said to his student Timothy, Study to shew thyself approved unto God, a workman that needeth not to be ashamed, rightly dividing the word of truth. (2 Tim 2:15). This still applies today.

READING

Reading has historically been considered the fundamental vocational skill for a person to get and keep ahead, or to change jobs. Reading exposes you to the ideas of great men and women and how they were able to attain to great heights. One man of God says you are not ready for the race of life, until you lay hold on relevant information via reading. You need to appreciate the value of information in your quest for success. Your reading should be purposeful. You should read to gather the secrets that have made other men champions. The servant never traded with his talent possibly because he never read about investments and how he could make his money work for him. Better still how he could improve upon his talent. So he did not even think of putting it into the bank to earn some interest. No matter the field you are in you can become better at what you do by reading about what other people have said.

PROBLEM SOLVING

Problem-solving skills include the ability to recognize and define problems, invent and implement solutions, and track and evaluate results. Creative thinking not only requires the ability to understand problem-solving techniques, but also to transcend logical and sequential thinking, making the leap to innovation. Unresolved problems create dysfunctional relationships in societies. You are either a problem solver or a creator of one. The greatness of any employee is in their ability to find solutions to problems that arises on the job. This is what God expects of us. Don't be like the servant who goes to hide somewhere and appears later to tell his master he was afraid to solve problems literally - leading to non-performance.

CHAPTER TWO

The Power of A Dream

Where there is no revelation, the people cast off restraint;
but happy is he who keeps the law.
—Proverbs 29:18

I believe that each of us has a dream placed in the heart. This is not about winning a jackpot lottery which mostly stems from our desire to escape the present harsh economic conditions the world is currently experiencing. It's about a vision deep inside that speaks to the very soul; that tells us what we were born to do. It draws on our talents and gifts and appeals to our highest ideals. It is inseparably linked to our purpose in life. The dream starts us on the success journey. A dream does many things for us;

- A dream gives us direction
- A dream increases our potential
- A dream helps us prioritise
- A dream adds value to our work
- A dream predicts our future

The parable of the talents gives us three different people with different mindsets - which were to maximise the talents they were given but out of the three one failed. The reason for his failure can be attributed to the lack of a dream, a vision or a purpose. However, the other two saw themselves achieving what they had conceived in their heart and finally ended up maximising the talents they were given. Remember, your vision or dream will help attract the needed resources to achieve. Have a dream and work it

Oliver Wendell Holmes said, "the great thing in this world is not so much where we are but in what direction we are moving." This means one can pursue his dream wherever he is in life. Begin to pursue you dream today and don't wait for things to be better because chances are that they will not. Esther had a dream to see the liberation of the Jewish community during her reign, Ruth had a dream of following Naomi until death, the Wright brothers had dream of flying in the sky and Jesus, our Saviour, had a dream of redeeming us from the bondage of sin. What is your dream? Dare to dream and act on that dream for therein lies your opportunity to do more for God and humanity.

CHAPTER THREE

Without Delay

Every day of delay leaves a day more to repent
of and a day less to repent in.

Procrastination it is said is the thief of time. Many a time, we defer and subsequently forsake particular assignments because we put it off till a later date. The servant who received five talents (the Bible says) immediately went and traded with it. He treated his business with a sense of urgency and made good use of his time. We must treat our purpose and assignment as such. Time does not wait for you, it moves no matter what you are doing but can only be filled with key responsibilities. Eclessiastes 9:10 says "Whatever your hand finds to do, do it with your might; for there is no work or device or knowledge or wisdom in the grave where you are going."

Some key decisions you must not delay on;

1. The decision to accept Jesus Christ as your Lord and personal saviour and to follow His steps
2. The decision to find out your God given assignment and to stay within the confines of that assignment.
3. The decision to depend on no one to educate you or cultivate the habit of reading
4. The decision to save and invest some money for you never know when the season of scarcity will come.
5. The decision to pray daily concerning the fulfilment of your assignment.
6. The decision to start that business, ministry or institution.
7. The decision to serve in the church and for that matter the ministry
8. The decision to be good at whatever your chosen field is.
9. The decision to think through situations and not hurriedly decide on them.

10. The decision to live a healthy life with regards to what you eat, drink and to exercise regularly.
11. The decision to have mentors and to wisely follow after the things they do.
12. The decision to persist, work hard and take care of your family.

CHAPTER FOUR

The Spirit of Ownership

One of the things that has limited many people when it comes to performance, achievement, taking care of things, doing their work with excellence and producing results is they don't see the work (or company) as theirs. This is seen in the attitude some people exhibit in the execution of their duties at their work places either in the market, church, offices etc. Today many organisations have the adopted ESOP (Employee Share Ownership Plan) to make employees see the business as theirs thus inducing them to work hard to maximise shareholder value. This is a clear case of making the employees cultivate the spirit of ownership. The kind of spirit that sees things as their own before they actually become theirs.

Many organisations, businesses and families are suffering today because the people that run these entities don't see them as theirs and as such manage them carelessly. Church members think the church belongs to the pastor and that he must come early to start services.Employees think that the business belongs to the chief executive officer and that he must be at work on time and leave late as well while expecting higher salaries from him. Young people think they are schooling for their parents and as such do not give the necessary attention to their education. Why do these things happen? The answer is simple. People do not treat things as theirs. In the parable of the talents, the servant with the one talent saw it as his master's and as such did not treat that talent as his own.

CEO OF YOUR LIFE

Begin to think of yourself as a CEO; as a leader; the one who makes all the decisions about your life. Like Adam in the garden, you have the power to subdue and have dominion, and you must know that the earth is the Lord's but God has given you the task to run it. I like this understanding of ownership and stewardship. God owns your life, but you take care for it. You are the one sitting as the executive chair of your life and if you don't guide your personal corporation, then you will miss the chance to reap the dividends for which you were created. In the parable of the talents, the servant who was given one talent never thought this way otherwise he wouldn't have gone to hide his talent. The servants that received five and two talents respectively worked as if the talents belong to them but not so with the one who received one talent. Understand that you are the leader of your life; you must see and treat things as your own.

WHY PEOPLE DON'T TREAT THINGS AS THEIR OWN

1. They don't know that stewardship is ownership
2. They live cautiously
3. They are afraid to venture out to the unknown
4. They are the people who have been compelled to be perpetual hewers of wood and drawers of water.
5. They work for pay.

Secrets of Ownership

1. If something is your own, you give and invest into it.
2. When something is yours, you patiently wait for the fruit.
3. You are faithful with what belongs to others.
4. You must realise you will give an account of whatever you have been given
5. You receive fulfilment in what is your own.

Job Mentality versus Business Ownership Mentality

The differences:

Business owners think "outside the box".

One of the most important qualities of business owners is that they are very open-minded and are radical thinkers. They are always challenging the status quo and finding what most people would call "loop-holes" in the economy. Observe the masses and do the opposite is the battle-cry for the modern day entrepreneur. This takes a certain amount of courage and gall. The biggest reason why so many people are more comfortable with a job is because it is safer.

Now based on the state of the economy today I would argue that job security is not what it used to be, but for now let us presume having a job is less risky than owning a business. The challenge for most people to make the transition from employee to business owner is that they are used to making money by showing up to work and getting a paycheck. That is how they have been preconditioned to make money so any other form of creating income to them just doesn't make sense to even bother with.

Robert Kiyosaki has stated that he never pays his kids for doing any chores around the house because he doesn't want them getting "addicted" to one specific process or method of making money. Showing up to work and trading time for money believe it or not is just ONE way of creating income. Some people would point out that there are many more people working than are in business so why not just join the masses. This is correct. However, understand that just because a million people are doing the same thing doesn't make it the right thing to do! Business owners think very differently from employees. This explains why the servants who received five and two talents respectively performed better than the one who received a talent because they looked for ways to maximize their talents. They thought differently.

BUSINESS OWNERS ARE NOT SCARED OF FAILURE; THEY EMBRACE IT.

This should go without saying but business owners are very tough, mentally. The nature of the job world is that there is very little room for failure. This is partly because if you make mistakes your supervisor also gets reprimanded for your inefficiency so it only makes sense that they take it out on you as well. What this tends to do is produce complacency in employees who would rather not push the envelope and get ridiculed for trying something different that didn't work. In business, however, you are taught to embrace failure as your friend. Success and failure are like Siamese twins; you can't get one without the other.

Business owners understand this and are more likely to embrace mistakes and failures because most times they answer to no one else but themselves. Failing is also the only way to learn in business especially if you have no mentorship or coaching along the way. Thomas Edison when first attempting to invent the light bulb stated about his failed attempts that he had not failed, but just found 10,000 ways that won't work. That's ownership mentality. They understand the opposite of success is not failure, it's quitting. The servant who was given one talents did not make use of his talent because he was afraid of failure and for that matter fear of risk. *And I was afraid, and went and hid thy talent in the earth: lo, there thou hast that is thine. (Matt. 25:25).* If you are going to succeed in whatever field God has called you, you have to be a risk taker. In other words have the kind of faith that says even when God does not show up, I will still trust in Him.

BUSINESS OWNERS KNOW WHO TO LISTEN TO.

Business owners are very careful who or what they let into their heads. This is not to say that they are arrogant, but they understand their mind is the most important thing they have. Charlie "Tremendous" Jones is quoted as saying that "Who you will be in the next five years will be a culmination of two things: the people you associate with and the books you read". Most of us if we have a reading habit can control that half of the equation, but people are a little tougher. And usually, family and friends have the biggest influence on the way we think.

If you take a look at the families of most employees you will most likely see that they have parents who are also still working, their grandparents worked, their great-grandparents worked, their cousins, siblings, aunts, pets, EVERYBODY had or has a job. No wonder they think the way they go about creating income. If you also examine a business owner you will see that the family is made up of a variety of entrepreneurial minded people with maybe a few of them going into business for themselves.

Business owners understand that when it comes to making money, you cannot learn anything from someone who does not have what you want. If you are driven by financial independence and security, then taking advice from someone who is driven by benefits is not going to help you. Be careful who you listen to. As a rule of thumb, take a look and see if they are in life where you want to be in the future. If the answer is no, run!

The parable of the talents introduces us to two different mindsets i.e. thinking which is present oriented and that which is future oriented. The present oriented thinkers most times do things to satisfy them in the now and do not think of tomorrow. On the other hand, the future oriented thinker's actions are forward looking. The servants who received good remarks from their master teaches us the importance of reading and right association because I believe they associated with the right people in their community and read about what others have done so they can do better in their assignments.

CHAPTER FIVE

Are You An Architect or Firefighter?

Remember, your goal is to cultivate a solution-oriented attitude that you bring into play all the time.
—John C. Maxwell

An architect is a creator or someone who invents something. In other words, they plan and design what they see in their mind's eye. Every believer has this grace and for that matter the gift of creativity to design through the eyes of faith, their future. Hebrews 11:1 says "...now faith is the substance of things hoped for, the evidence of things not seen". Like the architect, there must be the gathering of all that is necessary for the building process and that is giving substance to things hoped for, though not seen.

Every architect knows exactly how they want their building to be like. They don't set out to design houses or skyscrapers that will collapse in a year or two. For this reason, they design structures that are resilient to any storm or crisis. This makes them very future oriented. However, fire fighters are not so because they only respond to crisis. The sound of their sirens tells you there is a crisis of a fire outbreak somewhere in town. This attitude of responding to crisis does not augur well for proper planning. If we are to make the most of our talents and turn out returns on them, we must operate with the mindset of an architect and not that of a fire fighter.

According to John Perkins, there are three kinds of people in our society: those who can't see or refuse to see the problem; those who see the problems and because they didn't personally create them are content to blame someone else; and those who see the problems and though they didn't create them are willing to assume personal responsibility for solving them. The latter is what we should all strive to become.

CHAPTER SIX

The Future Belongs to Risk Takers

"Security is mostly a superstition.
It does not exist in nature, nor do the
children of men as a whole experience it.
Avoiding danger is no safer in the long run
than outright exposure. Life is either a daring
adventure or nothing."
—Helen Keller

The future belongs to risk takers, not security seekers. Life is paradoxical in the sense that the more you seek security, the less of it you have. But the more you seek opportunity, the more likely it is that you will achieve the security that you desire. Begin today what you will want to become or do tomorrow. Everything you will ever do involves some risk. It could be driving, crossing the road, investing, starting a business or an institution etc but taking the risk can be meaningful than to remain on the sideline and do nothing.

The servant with one talent told his master he was afraid and went to hid that which was given to him to work with. This servant can virtually be described as an unadventurous man who looks for safety or security despite the fact that they can be better off by taking an audacious step. The two other servants were daring and that took them to their next level i.e. becoming part-owners of their master's business. Take some calculated risk and move forward or remain at where you are in life. The bible testifies of David in 1 Samuel 17:28-58 of the risk he took that landed him in King Saul's palace and the privileges he got as a result of it.

And Eliab his eldest brother heard when he spake unto the men; and Eliab's anger was kindled against David, and he said, Why camest thou down hither? and with whom hast thou left those few sheep in the wilderness? I know thy pride, and the naughtiness of thine heart; for thou art come down that thou mightest see the battle. And David said, What have I now done? Is there not a cause? And he turned from him toward another, and spake after the same manner: and the people answered him again after the former manner. And when the words were heard which David spake, they rehearsed them before Saul: and he sent for him.

And David said to Saul, Let no man's heart fail because of him; thy servant will go and fight with this Philistine. And Saul said to David, Thou art not able to go against this Philistine to fight with him: for thou art but a youth, and he a man of war from his youth. And David said unto Saul, Thy servant kept his father's sheep, and there came a lion, and a bear, and took a lamb out of the flock: And I went out after him, and smote him, and delivered it out of his mouth: and when he arose against me, I caught him by his beard, and smote him, and slew him. Thy servant slew both the lion and the bear: and this uncircumcised Philistine shall be as one of them, seeing he hath defied the armies of the living God. David said moreover, The LORD that delivered me out of the paw of the lion, and out of the paw of the bear, he will deliver me out of the hand of this Philistine.

And Saul said unto David, Go, and the LORD be with thee. And Saul armed David with his armour, and he put an helmet of brass upon his head; also he armed him with a coat of mail. And David girded his sword upon his armour, and he assayed to go; for he had not proved it. And David said unto Saul, I cannot go with these; for I have not proved them. And David put them off him. And he took his staff in his hand, and chose him five smooth stones out of the brook, and put them in a shepherd's bag which he had, even in a scrip; and his sling was in his hand: and he drew near to the Philistine. And the Philistine came on and drew near unto David; and the man that bare the shield went before him. And when the Philistine looked about, and saw David, he disdained him: for he was but a youth, and ruddy, and of a fair countenance.

And the Philistine said unto David, Am I a dog, that thou comest to me with staves? And the Philistine cursed David by his gods. And the Philistine said to David, Come to me, and I will give thy flesh unto the fowls of the air, and to the beasts of the field. Then said David to the Philistine, Thou comest to me with a sword, and with a spear, and with a shield: but I come to thee in the name of the LORD of hosts, the God of the armies of Israel, whom thou hast defied. This day will the LORD deliver thee into mine hand; and I will smite thee, and take thine head from thee; and I will give the carcases of the host of the Philistines this day unto the fowls of the air, and to the wild beasts of the earth; that all the earth may know that there is a God in Israel. And all this assembly shall know that the LORD saveth not with sword and spear: for the battle is the LORD'S, and he will give you into our hands.

And it came to pass, when the Philistine arose, and came and drew nigh to meet David, that David hasted, and ran toward the army to meet the Philistine. And David put his hand in his bag, and took thence a stone, and slang it, and smote the Philistine in his forehead, that the stone sunk into his forehead; and he fell upon his face to the earth. So David prevailed over the Philistine with a sling and with a stone, and smote the Philistine, and slew him; but there was no sword in the hand of David. Therefore David ran, and stood upon the Philistine, and took his sword, and drew it out of the sheath thereof, and slew him, and cut off his head therewith. And when the Philistines saw their champion was dead, they fled.

And the men of Israel and of Judah arose, and shouted, and pursued the Philistines, until thou come to the valley, *and to the gates of Ekron. And the wounded of the Philistines fell down by the way to Shaaraim, even unto Gath, and unto Ekron. And the children of Israel returned from chasing after the Philistines, and they spoiled their tents. And David took the head of the Philistine, and brought it to Jerusalem; but he put his armour in his tent. And when Saul saw David go forth against the Philistine, he said unto Abner, the captain of the host, Abner, whose son is this youth? And Abner said, As thy soul liveth, O king, I cannot tell. And the king said, Enquire thou whose son the stripling is. And as David returned from the slaughter of the Philistine, Abner took him, and brought him before Saul with the head of the Philistine in his hand. And Saul said to him, Whose son art thou, thou young man? And David answered, I am the son of thy servant Jesse the Bethlehemite.*

CHAPTER SEVEN

Faithful Over A Few Things

Thus he left all that he had in Joseph's hand, and he did not know what he had except for the bread which he ate. Now Joseph was handsome in form and appearance.Gen 39:6

Moreover it is required in stewards that one be found faithful.1 Cor. 4:2

Oh, love the LORD, all you His saints! For the LORD preserves the faithful, And fully repays the proud person. Psalm 31:23

Most men will proclaim each his own goodness, But who can find a faithful man? Prov.20:6

A faithful man will abound with blessings, But he who hastens to be rich will not go unpunished. Prov.28:20

And I appointed as treasurers over the storehouse

Shelemiah the priest and Zadok the scribe, and of the Levites, Pedaiah; and next to them was Hanan the son of Zaccur, the son of Mattaniah; for they were considered faithful, and their task was to distribute to their brethren. Neh. 13:13

His lord said to him, 'Well done, good and faithful servant; you were faithful over a few things, I will make you ruler over many things. Enter into the joy of your lord.'Matt.25:21

CHAPTER EIGHT

The Matthew Effect

*For to everyone who has, more will be given, and he will
have abundance; but from him who does not have, even
what he has will be taken away.*
—Matthew 25:29

The professional soccer player starts out a little bit
better than his peers who just play on the streets or be-
hind his backyard because he gets the opportunity that
makes that difference a bit bigger, and that edge in turn
leads to another opportunity, which makes the initial-
ly small difference bigger still and on and on until the
soccer player is a genuine outlier. But he didn't start out
that way. He started out just a little bit better.

The sociologist Robert Merton famously called this phenomenon the 'Matthew Effect' after the New Testament Gospel of Matthew. It further states, those who are successful are most likely to be given the kinds of special opportunities that lead to further success. In like manner, the three servants in the parable of the talents were given equal opportunity but only two exemplified the Matthew Effect because they exposed themselves to hard work coupled with talent and passion in the assignments. And so they moved from managing few resources to many. . What qualifies you to be ruler over many things or command more resources is getting better at what you do, faithfully increasing your return on life and avoid being a wicked and lazy servant.

GEOGRAPHY MATTERS

Where you are determines who sees you, so choose carefully where you position yourself geographically. Where you are also determines the kind of training or opportunities for expansion of capabilities you get. If you choose to live in an environment where negativity is the order of the day, you will become same and the opposite is also true. So choose to tap into great minds and get exposure for greater works. David found himself in the palace of King Saul to play a harp and that exposed him to how the King runs the nation of Israel.

Therefore Saul sent messengers to Jesse, and said, "Send me your son David, who is with the sheep. And Jesse took a donkey loaded with bread, a skin of wine, and a young goat, and sent them by his son David to Saul. So David came to Saul and stood before him. And he loved him greatly, and he became his armorbearer. Then Saul sent to Jesse, saying, "Please let David stand before me, for he has found favor in my sight. And so it was, whenever the spirit from God was upon Saul, that David would take a harp and play it with his hand. Then Saul would become refreshed and well, and the distressing spirit would depart from him. (2 Sam.16:19-23)

These scriptures provide proof that David spent days in King Saul's palace and in that setting he had the chance to learn from the King as well as enhance his skills. This helped him during his reign as the King of Israel.

FROM FEW TO *Many*

YOU NEED INTERPRETERS

Interpreters are people that are able to interprete dreams and visions. In other words they serve as mentors who see your future before you do. The butler and baker needed Joseph when they dreamt. You need an interpreter to help you understand the dreams and visions God has placed in you. These are people who also serve as door openers who expose you to great things and go the extra mile with you.

THE LAW OF ASSOCIATION

Association is necessary for impartation and empowerment. The people you associate with determine the kind of advice, instruction or training you receive.1 Corth.15:33 says "Do not be deceived: "Evil company corrupts good habits." We associate to receive impartation to reproduce what has been imparted and be empowered to do that which we have received. Choose carefully whom you associate with.

CHAPTER NINE

The Points of Difference

A winner is someone who recognizes his God-given talents,
works his tail off to develop them into skills, and uses these
skills to accomplish his goals.
—Larry Bird

There are attributes or key characteristics consumers strongly associate with a brand, positively evaluate and believe they could not find to the same extent with a competing brand i.e. points where you are claiming superiority or exclusiveness over other products in the category. This is a term generally used by marketers in selling their products to customers. The points of difference are what make a product different from that of its competitors. It needs not be better or worse than what the competitor does. Just different.P.O.D could be information or a new slant that the customer doesn't know and with this new and different information, the customer can change his mind without any criticism. Everybody has a point of difference in life and it is this which makes you stand apart from others.

In Jer.1:4-5, God informs Jeremiah of his assignment and call to the nations as a prophet which sets the tone for his point of difference.

Then the word of the LORD came to me, saying; Before I formed you in the womb I knew you; Before you were born I sanctified you; I ordained you a prophet to the nations."

Jeremiah's P.O.D was to proclaim the mind of God to the people of Israel. Yours may be an educator; a pastor who counsels and trains young people; a teacher who is gifted in the teaching of mathematics to grade 4 pupils; a leader who is called to lead a group etc. All these confirms your points of difference and separates you from others. A critical look at the three servants in the parable of the talents brings out their points of difference and the fact that they were each given different amounts means their master knew how different each one was.

In another perspective, the servant who had the highest amount can be classified as having a great point of difference because it was by virtue of this that he was able to increase his money or talents by one hundred percent and the same can be said of the second servant but not the last one. However between the first and second, the amount given to each were not the same indicating the two had a point of difference which made the former receive more than the latter. This is shown below in what I call *the three servants points of difference table:*

THE SERVANT	AMOUNT GIVEN	RETURN ON INVESTMENT (ROI)	RECOMMENDA- TION
1st Servant	$5,000.00	100%	Promoted to a Partner
2nd Servant	$2,000.00	100%	Promoted to A Partner
3rd Servant	$1,000.00	0%	Demoted

Everyone buys a product for a purpose or because of the problem that product will solve. Similarly, we are God's product fashioned to solved a particular problem or fulfil a specific reason. How we seek to discover, apply ourselves to continuous improvement and maximise the gifts and talents wired in us brings out our points of difference. From table, the last servant produced nothing because he never thought he was to fulfil a purpose with what was given and for that matter make use of his point of difference.

The bible says of Jesus in John 3:14-17, *And as Moses lifted up the serpent in the wilderness, even so must the Son of Man be lifted up, that whoever believes in Him should not perish but have eternal life. For God so loved the world that He gave His only begotten Son, that whoever believes in Him should not perish but have everlasting life. For God did not send His Son into the world to condemn the world, but that the world through Him might be saved.* This means Jesus' mandate and mission was to save the world and still is. That is our Lord's point of difference; the only saviour of the world. What is yours?

CHAPTER TEN

Live Out Your God Given Dream

To find his place and fill it is success for a man.

Alexander Woolcott, one of the most famous alumni of Hamilton College, New York, was asked to give a major address at the college's centennial celebration. Woolcott gave a memorable speech which began with these words: "I send my greetings today to all my fellow alumni of Hamilton College, scattered all over the world. Some of you are successes, and some of you are failures - only God knows which are which!" This is a wonderful reminder to us that in our measurement of success and failure in relation to living out our God given dream, "God's thoughts are not our thoughts, nor are our ways God's ways. As the heavens are higher than the earth, so are God's ways higher than our ways, and God's thoughts than our thoughts" (Isaiah 55:8-9 paraphrase). This is the lesson that can be gleaned from the parable of the talents and the overambitious disciples, James and John.

If there is one thing we know for sure about predestination it is this: God created everyone for success. God did not create anyone for failure. But what do success and failure mean? For most people, like James and John, success means to be head of the pack. To succeed means to excel. Success is measured by comparing one's achievements against the achievements of one's "competitors." That is why James and John go to Jesus and ask not that they be granted a place in his kingdom but that they be granted "to sit, one at your right hand and one at your left, in your glory" (Mark 10:37). "You do not know what you are asking," Jesus says to them (verse 38), and then proceeds to teach them a new understanding of success.

LIVE OUT YOUR GOD GIVEN DREAM

For Jesus success means people realizing and fulfilling God's dream for them, contrary to popular thinking, that anybody can be anything. Before people come into this world, divine providence has already crafted a dream for each person to live out. We do not come into life to write our own job description, we come with a divine job description in our hands and with the physical and mental traits necessary to get the job done. That is what the parable of the talents teaches us. The master (God) needed a singular job to be done, that of trading with their talents, be productive and He fully equipped them specifically to do the job. Each of the three servants had a mandate only they could fulfill. This is why Jesus tells James and John that, "to sit at my right hand or at my left is not mine to grant, but it is for those for whom it has been prepared" (verse 40). Those who take the steps to live out their God given dream.

Does this mean that God has already determined, from the word go, the outcome of our earthly existence? No. God has an intended destination for which He created you and me. This is predestination. But whether you and I attain this destination or not depends on how we cooperate with God's grace. The three servants were all given talents according to their ability but were not set out for failure except, they chose to be profitable or not. To say that whatever people are or do in life is what God created them to be and do is determinism. The Bible teaches predestination (God has something in mind for creating you and me) but does not teach determinism (whatever we are or do is what God has predestined for us). God gives us free will to cooperate with divine grace or not. That is why, even though God predestined Mary to be the mother of our Saviour, when the time came for her to accomplish this mission, God sent an angel to seek her cooperation. She is a perfect example of one who lived out her God given dream, so were the two profitable servants because she courageously said yes to the word of God detailing to her what Providence has in store for her.

The servant who was given a talent, James and John, on the other hand, represent the New Age anyone-could-be-anything mentality characteristic of our times. The new vision of success that Jesus teaches, on the contrary, encourages mutual cooperation and the contentment of realizing that we can all be successful because God has created every one of us for something different like the three servants. God has enough dreams to go round, a different dream for everyone; a different success story for everyone. Our aim in life should be to discover and live God's dream for us. Herein lays our true success.

CHAPTER ELEVEN

Be Preservatives

Salt is good: but if the salt has lost its saltiness,
wherewith will ye season it? Have salt in yourselves,
and have peace one with another.
—Mark 9:49

A preservative is a natural or synthetic substance that is added to products such as foods, pharmaceuticals, paints, biological samples, wood, etc. to prevent decomposition by microbial growth or by undesirable chemical changes. Having salt in ourselves means that we retain in ourselves those precious qualities that will make us a blessing to one another, and to all around us.

Salt is good … To make meat savoury, and keep flesh

from corrupting; and so is the grace of God, to season men's hearts, make their discourse savoury, and preserve them from the corruption of sin: and so men may be made partakers of the grace of God; they are good and useful to others, both by their words and actions, and especially ministers of the Gospel, who are "the salt of the earth."

See that ye have at all times the preserving principle of Divine grace in your hearts, and give that proof of it which will satisfy your own minds, and convince or silence the world.

Have the preserving, purifying principle always; the principles of denying yourselves, of suppressing pride, ambition, contention, etc., and thus you will be an acceptable offering to God.

CHAPTER TWELVE

Self Realisation In Christ

*Christ is the only transforming power there is and
we strive in vain without Him whether we are
building a life or a country.*
—Rosalie Mills Appleby

There is an old African fable about how the duck learnt to swim. Duck and Hen lived together in a house by the seaside. Their food was the rotten fish that fishermen threw away. Everyday they saw Heron swimming up and down the sea, catching and eating fresh fish. This made Duck desire so much to have some fresh fish. But Hen said to Duck, "Why do you desire what you can't have? The Heron is a sea-bird. Her body is light. We are land-birds and land-birds do not swim. If you enter the sea with this your heavy body you will sink like a stone and that will be the end of you." Duck believed Hen. So they went on eating their rotten fish. But this did not stop Duck's hunger and inborn desire for fresh fish.

One very hot and humid day, Duck could eat nothing at all because the rotten fish smelled so bad. She just went and sat by herself, quietly looking at the sea. In a moment Heron came sailing by and saw Duck in such a pitiable condition. Heron asked what the matter was and Duck told him everything: how she always longed to swim and eat fresh fish but, unfortunately, the Creator had made her a heavy land-bird. It was then that Heron explained to Duck that sometime in the past, even he himself was not a swimmer, but that he was forced by hunger to jump into the sea and then he discovered he could swim. Heron invited Duck to jump into the sea and give it a try but Duck was afraid. With more encouragement from Heron, Duck overcame her fears and stepped into the sea. To her surprise Duck saw that she was not sinking; she was floating. With time Duck learnt to swim well and catch and eat as much fresh fish as she wanted.

You see, Duck was not just a land-bird. She was equally a sea-bird. But as long as she believed that she was only a land-bird, she remained on the land and suffered want and privation. So the story is really about how the duck came to discover and realise her God-given identity and potential as a swimmer. It is about how the flower bud blossoms into the beautiful flower that it is destined to be. Similarly the story of Bartimaeus in today's gospel is about how a nobody begging by the roadside came to realise his God-given dignity as a human being and child of God; how he blossomed.

The story of the healing of blind Bartimaeus in Mark 10:46-52 has aroused the curiosity of bible scholars because this is about the only place in the Synoptic Gospels where the name of a person who was healed by Jesus is given. The name is mentioned not only once but twice: "Bartimaeus, son of Timaeus," first in Aramaic, then in Greek. This very unusual emphasis on the name is a clue that the name is important for the reader to understand the point Mark is trying to make in the story.

In the ancient Semitic world, a name was not just a label to identify a person. A name expressed the personality or destiny of a person. So what does Bartimaeus mean? Literally, it comes from the Aramaic and means "son/person of defilement." This could, therefore, be a nickname given to him because he was a blind beggar. Popular theology among the Hebrews held blindness to be a punishment from God for sin or defilement (John 9:34). But the Greek version of the name could also be understood as "son/person of honour". This would indicate the man's inner nature and destiny. By giving us the name Bartimaeus with its double meaning, Mark could be telling us that here is a man who is supposed to be a man of honour and dignity living in a state of dishonour and shame. What Jesus did for him, therefore, was not simply restoring his physical sight but, over and above that, restoring his God-given human dignity. We can liken it to what the Heron did for the Duck, enlightening and empowering someone to realize their God-given potential and dignity.

Like Duck by the seaside, or like Bartimaeus by

the wayside, are you sometimes bored, feeling that there must be more to life than you are getting at the moment? Do you sometimes feel like you are born to be a swimmer and yet here you are idly walking and eating rotten fish by the seaside? Do you sometimes feel, like Bartimaeus, that you should be following Jesus in his enthusiastic campaign to save the world and yet you find yourselves all day long doing nothing but the same boring routine of trying to find food? The good news is that Jesus is passing by. He can heal and take away whatever weakness or handicap that holds you down. Do not pay heed to friends who, like the Hen, will say that you are daydreaming. Bartimaeus did not heed to those who tried to dissuade him. Jesus is here to heal the blindness that has immobilized you, to empower and transform you from a passive bystander to His active and enthusiastic follower in an otherwise boring journey of life.

BIBLIOGRAPHY

Jakes, T.D. *Before You Do: Making Great Decisions That You Won't Regret.* Atria Books, A division of Simon & Schuster Inc.2008

Oyedepo, David O. *Success Systems.* Dominion Publishing House.2007

Murdock, Mike. *The Assignment; The Dream And The Destiny.* The Wisdom Centre. 1996

Munachi E. Ezeogu (2012). *Homily for 29th Sunday in Ordinary Time.* Retrieved from website; https://justme-homely.wordpress.com/2012/10/20/twenty-ninth-sunday-in-ordinary-time-year-b-3/

Pavelko, John H. (2009). *Discovering Our Sight.* Retrieved from http://www.crossroadspc.org/thebarrel/2009/1025.htm

Leonard, Liz (2017). *Job Mentality Vs Business Owner Mentality.* Retrieved from website: http://lizleonardfranchiseadvisor.com/2017/09/08/having-job-own-ing-business/

THE FUTURE BELONGS TO RISK TAKERS

www.ingramcontent.com/pod-product-compliance
Lightning Source LLC
Chambersburg PA
CBHW071240090426
42736CB00014B/3164